THE BIG BOOK OF

CAT TRIVIA

300 QUESTIONS

Contents

Introduction

Welcome to the captivating world of cats—a world filled with mystery, charm, and an undeniable connection with humans. But why cats? Why have these independent, sometimes mischievous creatures become such beloved companions in our homes and hearts? Whether it's their elegant movements, curious personalities, or the comforting sound of their purring, cats have long fascinated people across cultures and eras. Their unique blend of independence and affection is unlike any other animal, making them the perfect subject for a trivia book that celebrates all things feline.

The relationship between cats and humans dates back thousands of years. From their revered status in ancient Egypt, where they were worshipped as symbols of protection, to their roles as loyal companions in households around the world today, cats have always held a special place in our lives. Throughout history, they have served as both protectors, keeping pests at bay, and as symbols of mystery and magic. Over time, cats have evolved from being functional members of society to becoming cherished family members, continuing to win hearts with their distinctive behaviors.

To get you started on your journey into the fascinating world of cats, here are some fun facts: Did you know that cats can make over 100 different sounds, or that a cat's purr may have healing properties? Or that cats have been to space? There is so much to learn about our feline friends, and this trivia book is packed with interesting tidbits, surprising facts, and playful insights that will deepen your appreciation for these remarkable animals.

So whether you're a seasoned cat enthusiast or just curious about the world of cats, this book is sure to entertain, inform, and ignite your love for these incredible creatures.

Enjoy the journey!

Chapter 1: Feline History, Legends and Famous Cats

1. Where did the domestication of cats most likely begin?

a) South America
b) Fertile Crescent
c) France
d) China

2. What species of wildcat is considered the closest ancestor to domestic cats?
a) African wildcat (Felis lybica)
b) European wildcat (Felis silvestris)
c) Serval (Leptailurus serval)
d) Lynx (Lynx lynx)

3. Why were cats initially attracted to human settlements?
a) Humans started feeding them
b) They were used for hunting
c) They followed the scent of cooking meat
d) They were drawn to rodents attracted by stored grain

4. Approximately how long ago did cats first become domesticated?
a) 1,000 years ago
b) 4,000 years ago
c) 9,000 years ago
d) 15,000 years ago

5. Which ancient civilization is most famous for worshiping cats as sacred animals?
a) The Romans
b) The Greeks
c) The Egyptians
d) The Persians

6. What is the name of the ancient Egyptian goddess often depicted with a cat's head?
a) Bastet
b) Isis
c) Hathor
d) Sekhmet

7. Which of the following is NOT a theory on how domestic cats spread across the world?
a) They were carried by traders along ancient trade routes
b) Cats migrated on their own, traveling across land bridges

c) They were brought aboard ships to control rats and mice

d) Cats were deliberately bred and traded between kingdoms

8. What role did domestic cats play in ancient Egypt?

a) They were considered symbols of wealth

b) They were worshiped as gods

c) They were primarily hunters of rodents

d) They were used as guardians for temples

9. What evidence suggests cats were domesticated by early farmers?

a) Cat figurines in temples

b) Cat burials near human settlements

c) Cave paintings of cats

d) Skeletal remains found in ancient cities

10.Which genetic mutation is linked to the more sociable and less aggressive behavior seen in domestic cats compared to their wild counterparts?

a) A change in brain development genes

b) A mutation affecting hunting instincts

c) A change in vocalization patterns

d) A mutation related to muscle development

11. Which archaeological discovery in Cyprus provided evidence of early human-cat relationships?

a) Cat-shaped pottery
b) A cat buried alongside a human
c) Ancient cat mummification
d) Cave paintings of cats

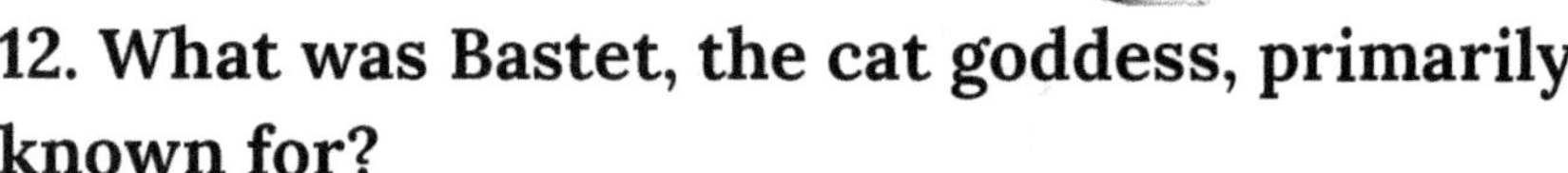

12. What was Bastet, the cat goddess, primarily known for?

a) Goddess of war and hunting
b) Goddess of protection, fertility, and home
c) Goddess of the sun and moon
d) Goddess of death and the afterlife

13. Why were cats considered sacred in Ancient Egypt?

a) They were believed to have magical healing powers
b) They symbolized the pharaoh's power
c) They protected homes from pests and represented the goddess Bastet
d) They were thought to control the weather

14. What would happen to a person who harmed or killed a cat in Ancient Egypt?

a) They were fined heavily
b) They were exiled from the community
c) They could face the death penalty
d) They had to pay a tax to the temple

15. How did Ancient Egyptians often show their reverence for cats?
a) By dressing them in royal garments
b) By mummifying cats and offering them to the gods
c) By making cats the symbol of the pharaoh
d) By naming their cities after cats

16. Which city in Ancient Egypt was known as the center of worship for the cat goddess Bastet?
a) Thebes
b) Memphis
c) Bubastis
d) Alexandria

17. What common practice did Egyptians believe would bring them favor from the gods?
a) Offering food to stray cats
b) Creating statues of cats in their homes
c) Wearing amulets with cat symbols
d) Donating gold to the temple of Bastet

18. Why did the Egyptian army reportedly lose a battle against the Persians at Pelusium in 525 BCE?
a) The Persians poisoned their food supply
b) The Persians used wild cats as a distraction
c) The Persians used cats on their shields, knowing Egyptians wouldn't harm them
d) The Egyptian army was ambushed at night

19. What was the primary material used to wrap cat mummies in ancient Egypt?
a) Linen
b) Papyrus
c) Wool
d) Cotton

20. What was a common depiction of Bastet in Ancient Egyptian art?
a) A woman with the head of a monkey
b) A woman with the head of a cat
c) A bird with a cat's tail
d) A woman holding a snake

21. In Norse mythology, which goddess is associated with cats?
a) Freyja
b) Hel
c) Frigg

d) Skadi

22. What is the significance of the black cat in European folklore?

a) It brings good luck
b) It is considered a witch's familiar and a bad omen
c) It symbolizes wealth and prosperity
d) It is a protector of the home

23. In Japanese folklore, what is the name of the cat that is said to bring good fortune?

a) Neko
b) Kawaii
c) Maneki-neko
d) Tora

24. What role do cats play in the Celtic mythology of the Selkies?

a) They are feared for their power over the seas
b) They guide lost souls to the afterlife
c) They are often depicted as shape-shifters
d) They protect fishermen from storms

25. In Persian mythology, what does the term "Shah of Cats" refer to?

a) The leader of a group of cats
b) The mythical giant cat that brings peace

c) A legendary cat believed to have magical powers
d) A revered figure in ancient cat worship

26. In folklore, what does a cat crossing your path typically signify?

a) Good fortune ahead
b) A warning of impending danger
c) The arrival of a messenger
d) An invitation to a gathering

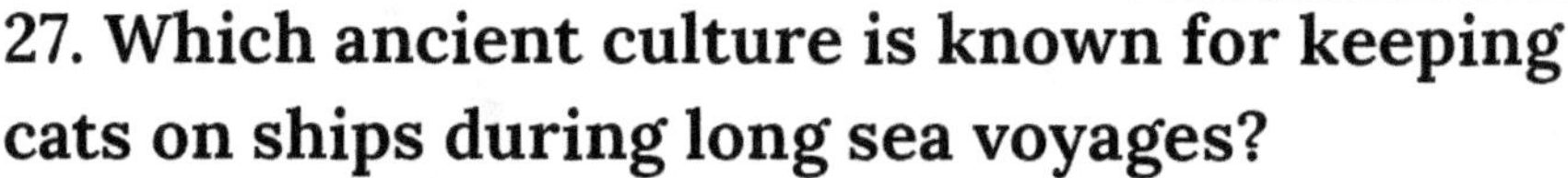

27. Which ancient culture is known for keeping cats on ships during long sea voyages?

a) The Vikings
b) The Phoenicians
c) The Greeks
d) The Romans

28. Name of the cat sent into space by the French government in 1963 as part of a research mission:

a) Felicette
b) Laika
c) Tibbles
d) Astrochatz

29. In Russian folklore, what does it mean if a cat washes its face in front of you?

a) Good luck is coming your way

b) You will soon have a visitor
c) It is a sign of bad news
d) You should prepare for a journey

30. In Japanese mythology, what happens when a cat lives for over 100 years?

a) It gains the ability to speak
b) It transforms into a powerful spirit known as a bakeneko
c) It becomes a guardian of the home
d) It receives magical powers to grant wishes

31. What was the name of the cat owned by President Bill Clinton?

a) Socks
b) Fluffy
c) Mr. Whiskers
d) Tom

32. Which famous artist was known for having a cat named Minou?

a) Pablo Picasso
b) Vincent van Gogh
c) Claude Monet
d) Leonardo da Vinci

33. What was the beloved cat of Ernest Hemingway, known for having six toes?

a) Siamese
b) Maine Coon
c) Polydactyl
d) Bengal

34. What was the name of the cat that belonged to Winston Churchill, often seen at his side?
a) Tom
b) Jock
c) Charlie
d) Tomkit

35. Which famous writer had a cat named Behemoth, featured in one of his novels?
a) Leo Tolstoy
b) Anton Chekhov
c) Mikhail Bulgakov
d) Fyodor Dostoevsky

36. How long did Felicette's space mission last during her flight in 1963?
a) 13 minutes
b) 30 minutes
c) 2 hours
d) 4 hours

37. Which poet is famous for their whimsical and affectionate portrayal of cats in the collection titled "Old Possum's Book of Practical Cats"?
a) Edgar Allan Poe
b) Robert Frost
c) T.S. Eliot
d) Langston Hughes

38. Which breed of cat was the composer Claude Debussy particularly fond of?
a) Persian
b) Siamese
c) Angora
d) Maine Coon

39. Which famous writer had the paw of his cat stuffed and mounted on a letter opener?
a) Mark Twain
b) Ernest Hemingway
c) Charles Dickens
d) F. Scott Fitzgerald

40. What type of cat did Salvador Dali adopt and name Babou?
a) Persian cat
b) Bengal cat
c) Colombian ocelot
d) Siamese cat

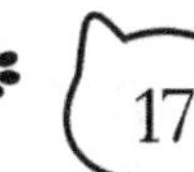

41. Which famous scientist had a cat named "Spithead", for which it is said that he invented the cat flap?
a) Albert Einstein
b) Isaac Newton
c) Charles Darwin
d) Nikola Tesla

42. What two means of refuge from the misery of life did Albert Einstein mention?
a) Books and music
b) Cats and dogs
c) Nature and art
d) Music and cats

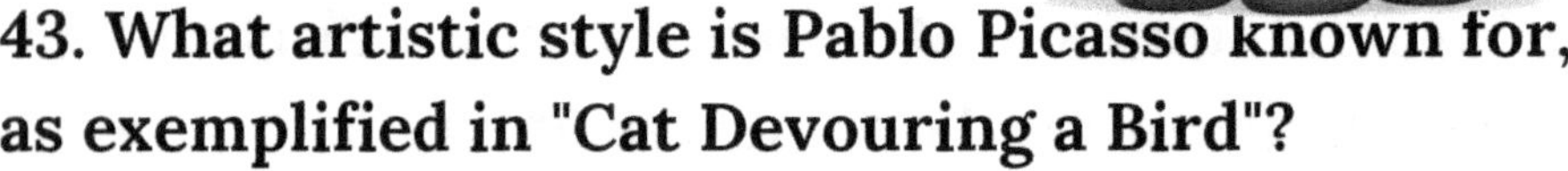

43. What artistic style is Pablo Picasso known for, as exemplified in "Cat Devouring a Bird"?
a) Impressionism
b) Cubism
c) Surrealism
d) Expressionism

44. What was the name of the famous cat that accompanied the British expedition to Antarctica in the early 1900s?
a) Snowball

b) Chippy
c) Captain
d) Iceberg

45. Which famous novel features a character named "Cat" who plays a pivotal role in the story?
a) The Catcher in the Rye
b) The Cat in the Hat
c) The Great Gatsby
d) Alice's Adventures in Wonderland

Chapter 2: Breeds and Their Unique Traits

46. What is the most recognizable feature of a Persian cat?
a) Long, flowing coat
b) Large ears
c) Spotted fur
d) Short tail

47. Which breed is known for its hairless appearance?
a) Siamese
b) Sphynx
c) Maine Coon
d) Burmese

48. The Maine Coon is famous for its:
a) Tiny size
b) Lack of fur
c) Long, bushy tail and large size
d) Striped fur

49. What is a key characteristic of a Siamese cat?
a) Blue eyes and vocal nature
b) Green eyes and quiet personality
c) Curly fur and small size
d) Stripes and large ears

50. Which breed has the unique trait of folded ears?
a) Scottish Fold
b) Ragdoll
c) Burmese
d) Abyssinian

51. The Ragdoll cat gets its name because of its:
a) Ability to jump high
b) Calm and floppy nature when picked up
c) Color-changing coat
d) Short legs

52. Which cat breed is often called a "gentle giant"?
a) Maine Coon
b) Sphynx
c) Russian Blue
d) Bengal

53. Bengal cats are known for their:

a) Speckled or marbled coat resembling wild cats
b) Blue eyes and small size
c) Long, silky coat
d) Hairless bodies

54. The Abyssinian breed is notable for which coat pattern?

a) Ticked coat (agouti)
b) Striped coat
c) Solid colors
d) Spotted coat

55. Which breed is famous for having short legs?

a) Munchkin
b) Bengal
c) Siamese
d) Ragdoll

56. The Savannah cat is a hybrid breed resulting from the crossbreeding of a domestic cat with what wild animal?

a) Leopard
b) Serval
c) Cheetah
d) Tiger

57. What is special about the Lykoi breed?
a) It has a wolf-like appearance due to partial hair
loss
b) It is completely hairless
c) It has long, curly fur
d) It changes color with the seasons

**58. Which rare breed is known for its curly fur and
is often referred to as the "poodle cat"?**
a) Cornish Rex
b) Sphinx
c) LaPerm
d) Selkirk Rex

59. The Turkish Van breed is unique for its love of:
a) Swimming
b) Climbing trees
c) Hunting
d) Sleeping

**60. What is a defining feature of the Japanese
Bobtail?**
a) Naturally short "pom-pom" tail
b) Spotted coat like a wild cat
c) Completely hairless body
d) Large, rounded eyes

61. The Serengeti cat was bred to resemble which wild animal?
a) Leopard
b) Cheetah
c) African Serval
d) Tiger

62. The Khao Manee is an exotic cat breed originally from which country?
a) Thailand
b) Egypt
c) Turkey
d) China

63. What is unique about the coat of the Cornish Rex?
a) It has no outer coat, just soft, wavy undercoat
b) It is completely hairless
c) It changes color with the seasons
d) It is striped like a tiger

64. Breed known for its muscular build, wild appearance and is one of the largest domestic cats:
a) Siamese
b) Bengal
c) Chausie
d) Norwegian Forest Cat

65. The Norwegian Forest Cat, a large and fluffy breed, originates from which region?
a) Scandinavia
b) Africa
c) Asia
d) South America

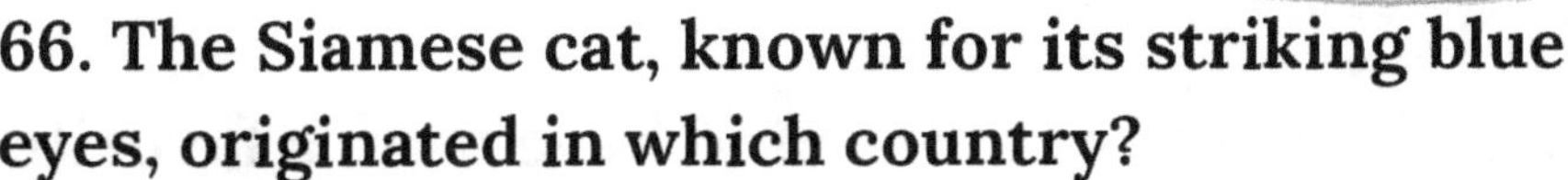

66. The Siamese cat, known for its striking blue eyes, originated in which country?
a) Thailand
b) India
c) Egypt
d) China

67. The Turkish Angora, a breed known for its silky fur, was first discovered in:
a) Turkey
b) Egypt
c) Greece
d) Italy

68. Which breed is thought to have descended from the sacred temple cats of Burma?
a) Burmese
b) Siamese
c) Birman
d) Turkish Van

69. The Chartreux breed, known for its plush gray coat, has historical ties to which European country?
a) France
b) Italy
c) Germany
d) Spain

70. Which breed is rumored to have been a favorite of French monks?
a) Chartreux
b) Russian Blue
c) Abyssinian
d) Maine Coon

71. The Russian Blue cat, with its short, dense, and bluish-gray coat, is believed to have originated from:
a) Russia
b) Egypt
c) China
d) India

72. The American Shorthair, one of the oldest cat breeds in the U.S., is believed to have been brought over by settlers from which country?

a) England
b) France
c) Spain
d) Germany

73. The British Shorthair is well-known for having which distinctive facial feature?

a) Large, round cheeks
b) Pointed nose
c) Long whiskers
d) Droopy eyes

74. What is unique about the coat of the LaPerm breed?

a) It has a curly, springy texture
b) It is hairless
c) It has stripes like a wild cat
d) It is extra thick and double-coated

75. The Bombay cat, often called a "mini-panther," was bred to resemble which wild animal?

a) Black panther
b) Tiger
c) Jaguar
d) Leopard

Chapter 3: Feline Biology and Behavior

76. Cats have a wider field of vision compared to humans. What is their field of view?
a) 200 degrees
b) 160 degrees
c) 230 degrees
d) 180 degrees

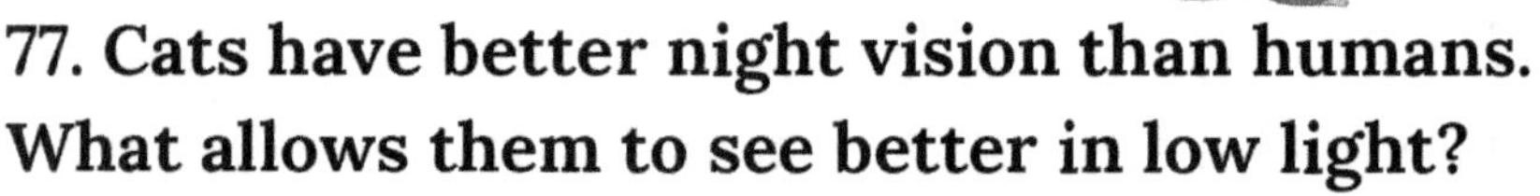

77. Cats have better night vision than humans. What allows them to see better in low light?
a) Extra rods in their eyes
b) Special cones in their eyes
c) Their large pupils
d) A reflective layer behind their retina called the tapetum lucidum

78. What colors are cats primarily able to see?
a) Red and yellow
b) Blue and green
c) Blue and gray
d) All colors, like humans

79. Why do cats have slit-shaped pupils?
a) To improve their peripheral vision
b) To control the amount of light entering their eyes
c) To focus better on distant objects
d) To protect their eyes from dust

80. Which of the following is true about a cat's depth perception?
a) Cats have poor depth perception because their eyes are set far apart
b) Cats have excellent depth perception due to their forward-facing eyes
c) Cats rely on whiskers more than vision for depth perception
d) Cats cannot perceive depth at all

81. At what frequency do cats typically purr?
a) 10-20 Hz
b) 25-150 Hz
c) 200-300 Hz
d) 500-600 Hz

82. Which of the following is a common reason for a cat's purring?
a) When they are happy
b) To communicate with other cats
c) To heal themselves

d) All of the above

83. True or False: Cats only purr when they are content.

a) True
b) False

84. How can purring benefit cats physically?

a) Purring helps relax their muscles
b) Purring helps in healing bones and tissues
c) Purring helps them sleep better
d) Purring aids in digestion

85. Why do kittens purr?

a) To attract their mother's attention
b) To show hunger
c) To bond with their mother while nursing
d) To indicate fear

86. What is the proper name for a cat's whiskers?

a) Vibrissae
b) Cilia
c) Dermis
d) Filaments

87. What is the primary function of a cat's whiskers?

a) Sensing sound
b) Detecting nearby objects and movements
c) Cooling down
d) Helping with balance

88. How many whiskers does the average cat have on each side of its face?

a) 8
b) 12
c) 16
d) 20

89. Where else, besides their face, do cats have whiskers?

a) On their neck
b) On their back
c) On their tail
d) On their forelegs

90. Can a cat sense changes in air currents using its whiskers?

a) True
b) False
c) Only when it is warm
d) Only smell changes

91. When a cat's tail is standing straight up, what does it usually indicate?
a) Fear
b) Confidence and friendliness
c) Hunger
d) Aggression

92. Why do cats knead with their paws?
a) It's a way of marking territory
b) To show dissatisfaction
c) To sharpen their claws
d) As a way to stretch their muscles

93. What does it mean when a cat's ears are flattened back against its head?
a) The cat is relaxed
b) The cat is curious
c) The cat is frightened or angry
d) The cat is playful

94. Why do cats often bring dead animals to their owners?
a) To show their hunting skills
b) As a gift or offering
c) To ask for praise
d) To scare away predators

95. What does it mean when a cat slowly blinks at you?

a) The cat is bored
b) The cat is tired
c) The cat is showing trust and affection
d) The cat is angry

96. On average, how many hours do cats sleep per day?

a) 8-10 hours
b) 12-16 hours
c) 16-20 hours
d) 20-24 hours

97. Why do cats sleep so much?

a) To conserve energy for hunting
b) To regulate their body temperature
c) To process food
d) To avoid predators

98. What is the term for the light sleep cats often enter, during which they are still alert to sounds and movements?

a) REM sleep
b) Light sleep
c) Paradoxical sleep
d) Cat nap

99. During REM sleep, what do cats commonly do?
a) Twitch their paws and whiskers
b) Purr loudly
c) Curl up tightly
d) Growl softly

100. How do cats' sleeping habits change as they age?
a) They sleep less as they get older
b) They sleep more as they get older
c) Their sleep patterns stay the same throughout life
d) They nap more frequently but for shorter periods

Chapter 4: Famous Cats in Pop Culture

101. Who is the author of the famous children's book "The Cat in the Hat"?
a) Beatrix Potter
b) J.K. Rowling
c) Dr. Seuss
d) Lewis Carroll

102. In the original "Puss in Boots" fairy tale, what role does the cat play?
a) A loyal companion
b) A trickster who helps his master rise to wealth and power
c) A villain
d) A pet who becomes royalty

103. What is the name of the cat in Lewis Carroll's Alice's Adventures in Wonderland?
a) Cheshire Cat
b) Tabby
c) Felix
d) Tom

**104. Who wrote a short story titled "The Black Cat,"
which explores themes of guilt and madness?**
a) Edgar Allan Poe
b) Mark Twain
c) Ernest Hemingway
d) F. Scott Fitzgerald

**105. In "Old Possum's Book of Practical Cats" by
T.S. Eliot, which musical was later based on these
feline characters?**
a) Cats
b) The Lion King
c) The Aristocats
d) Oliver!

**106. What is the name of the feline character in the
novel Coraline by Neil Gaiman?**
a) Puss
b) The Cat (it is unnamed)
c) Mogget
d) Salem

**107. In the "Warriors" series by Erin Hunter, what
are the main characters?**
a) Cats that form clans
b) Wild tigers in the jungle
c) Cats that can transform into humans

d) Space-traveling cats

108. In Harry Potter, what is the name of Hermione Granger's pet cat?

a) Crookshanks
b) Mrs. Norris
c) Snowball
d) Scabbers

109. What color was the Cheshire Cat from Alice's Adventures in Wonderland depicted by Disney?

a) Blue
b) Orange
c) Pink and purple stripes
d) Solid black

110. In Beatrix Potter's The Tale of Tom Kitten, what happens to Tom?

a) He gets lost in the garden
b) He ruins his clothes and gets scolded
c) He becomes king of the forest
d) He goes on an adventure with a dog

111. What is the name of the orange cat who loves lasagna and hates Mondays?

a) Felix
b) Tom

c) Garfield
d) Sylvester

112. In Tom and Jerry, who is Tom's main adversary?

a) A dog named Jerry
b) A bird
c) A mouse named Jerry
d) A cat named Felix

113. Which cartoon cat is famous for the catchphrase, "I tawt I taw a puddy tat"?

a) Felix the Cat
b) Top Cat
c) Sylvester
d) Tom

114. What color is Felix the Cat?

a) Orange
b) Black and white
c) Blue
d) Yellow

115. In The Simpsons, what is the name of the cartoon-within-a-cartoon that features a cat and mouse duo?

a) Tom and Jerry

b) CatDog

c) The Itchy & Scratchy Show

d) Sylvester & Tweety

116. What kind of cat is Heathcliff from the 1980s cartoon Heathcliff?

a) Stray alley cat

b) Domestic Siamese

c) Bengal cat

d) British Shorthair

117. In The Aristocats, what is the name of the mother cat?

a) Duchess

b) Marie

c) Tiger

d) Miss Kitty

118. What was Grumpy Cat's real name?

a) Tardar Sauce

b) Mr. Whiskers

c) Snowball

d) Smudge

119. Which viral cat was known for its pixelated body and rainbow trail?

a) Grumpy Cat

b) Nyan Cat

c) Lil BUB

d) Maru

120. Which famous internet cat is known for her toothless appearance and tongue permanently hanging out of the mouth?

a) Maru

b) Grumpy Cat

c) Smudge the Cat

d) Lil BUB

121. Which country is Maru, the internet-famous cat, from?

a) Japan

b) USA

c) UK

d) Australia

122. Fill in the name of the film with the name of an internet-famous cat "_ _ _ _'s Worst Christmas Ever".

a) Lil BUB

b) Nyan Cat

c) Grumpy Cat

d) Smudge

123. Which cat became famous for its ability to fit into tiny boxes and containers?
a) Grumpy Cat
b) Maru
c) Smudge
d) Lil BUB

124. In the Harry Potter movies, what type of cat is Professor McGonagall able to transform into?
a) Siamese
b) Tabby
c) Black
d) Calico

Chapter 5: Record-Breaking Cats

125. What is the name of the oldest recorded cat, who lived to be 38 years and 3 days old?
a) Creme Puff
b) Fluffy
c) Puss
d) Smokey

126. What breed holds the record for the tallest domestic cat ever recorded?
a) Maine Coon
b) Savannah
c) Ragdoll
d) Siamese

127. How much did Himmy, the world's heaviest recorded domestic cat, weigh when he set the record?
a) 15.5 kg (34 lbs)
b) 21.3 kg (46.8 lbs)
c) 18.7 kg (41 lbs)
d) 30.5 kg (67 lbs)

128. Which breed is the smallest domesticated cat in the world, in terms of size?

a) Singapura

b) Persian

c) Munchkin

d) Cornish Rex

129. What was the length of the longest recorded cat, Stewie the Maine Coon?

a) 90 cm (35.4 in)

b) 118 cm (46.6 in)

c) 123 cm (48.5 in)

d) 120 cm (47.2 in)

130. What is the most expensive cat breed, which can sell for as much as $125,000?

a) Bengal

b) Savannah

c) Ashera

d) Sphynx

131. How many kittens did the world record-holding cat, Dusty, give birth to during her lifetime?

a) 150

b) 218

c) 420

d) 312

132. What was the largest litter of kittens ever recorded by a single cat?

a) 14 kittens

b) 19 kittens

c) 20 kittens

d) 12 kittens

133. Which breed of cat is known for frequently having larger-than-average litters of kittens?

a) Ragdoll

b) Siamese

c) Cornish Rex

d) Persian

134. At what age did the world record-holding cat, Dusty, have her final litter of kittens?

a) 16 years old

b) 10 years old

c) 9 years old

d) 14 years old

135. Who holds the Guinness World Record for the cat with the longest fur?

a) Colonel Meow

b) Sophie

c) Fluffy

d) Fuzzy

136. What is the record for the most tricks performed by a cat in one minute?
a) 15 tricks
b) 26 tricks
c) 22 tricks
d) 18 tricks

137. Who is the holder of the loudest recorded purr by a domestic cat?
a) Smokey
b) Bella
c) Merlin
d) Whiskers

138. What is the loudest recorded purr by a domestic cat, measured in decibels?
a) 65 dB
b) 67.8 dB
c) 98 dB
d) 106 dB

139. What cat holds the Guinness World Record for the longest jump by a domestic cat, measuring 7 feet?
a) Waffle
b) Tiger
c) Mittens
d) Fluffy

140. Which cat holds the record for the most followed cat on Instagram?
a) Grumpy Cat
b) Nala
c) Nyan Cat
d) Smudge

Chapter 6: Cat Superstitions and Beliefs

141. In which country are black cats traditionally considered a symbol of good luck?
a) United States
b) Germany
c) Japan
d) Spain

142. In which culture is a black cat crossing your path seen as bad luck?
a) Irish
b) Greek
c) Indian
d) Egyptian

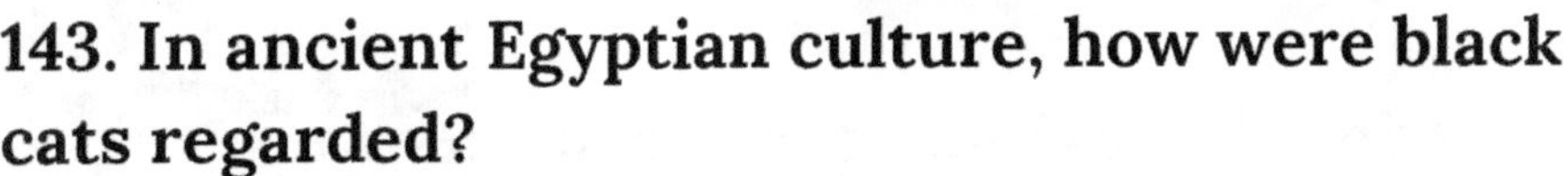

143. In ancient Egyptian culture, how were black cats regarded?
a) Sacred and protective
b) Mischievous tricksters
c) A symbol of famine
d) Creatures to be avoided

144. What does it mean in the United Kingdom if a black cat walks toward you?
a) Good fortune is on its way
b) You will soon face a difficult challenge
c) You will experience a loss
d) Nothing, it's neutral

145. In which profession are black cats often considered a symbol of protection and safety?
a) Sailors
b) Doctors
c) Teachers
d) Farmers

146. In European folklore, what were cats (especially black ones) often believed to be?
a) Reincarnated spirits
b) Witches in disguise
c) Omens of wealth
d) Spirits of protection

147. During the Middle Ages, black cats were associated with which supernatural event?
a) Full moon transformations
b) Nightmares
c) Witches' Sabbaths
d) Comets

148. In Norse mythology, what animal pulled the chariot of the goddess Freyja?
a) Horses
b) Cats
c) Wolves
d) Ravens

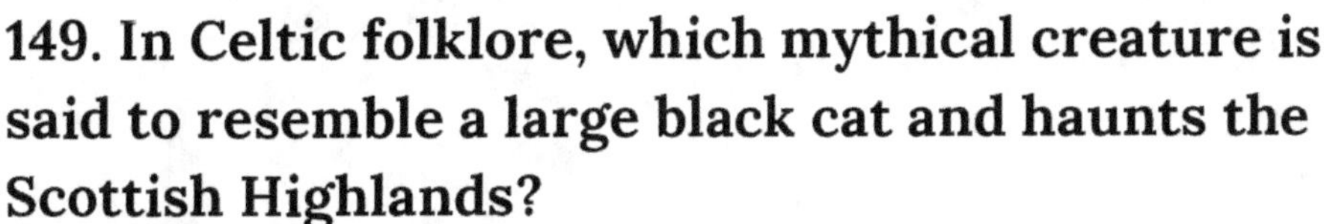

149. In Celtic folklore, which mythical creature is said to resemble a large black cat and haunts the Scottish Highlands?
a) Cat Sidhe
b) Banshee
c) Kelpie
d) Leanan Sidhe

150. In some cultures, it's believed that cats can see and communicate with what?
a) Guardian angels
b) Demons
c) Ghosts
d) Forest spirits

151. Which Asian culture views cats as symbols of good luck, particularly the "Maneki Neko" or beckoning cat?
a) Japanese
b) Chinese

c) Korean
d) Thai

152. In which European country were cats protected because they were believed to bring good harvests?
a) Italy
b) Russia
c) Poland
d) Latvia

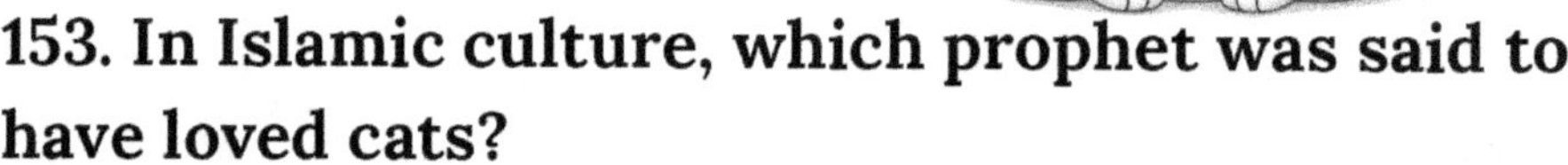

153. In Islamic culture, which prophet was said to have loved cats?
a) Prophet Muhammad
b) Prophet Ibrahim
c) Prophet Musa
d) Prophet Isa

154, Which sign of the Chinese zodiac is associated with the cat in Vietnamese astrology, but not in Chinese astrology?
a) Rabbit
b) Dragon
c) Goat
d) Ox

155. Which astrological sign is often compared to a

cat due to its playful, independent nature?

a) Leo

b) Gemini

c) Pisces

d) Sagittarius

156. In ancient Egyptian astrology, which cat-related goddess was believed to be connected to the sign of Leo?

a) Bastet

b) Sekhmet

c) Hathor

d) Nephthys

157. Which astrological element is often associated with cats due to their mysterious and aloof nature?

a) Water

b) Air

c) Fire

d) Earth

158. What kind of personality traits are commonly attributed to people born under the sign of Leo, which is symbolized by a lion, the cat's larger cousin?

a) Shy and reserved

b) Bold and confident

c) Mysterious and elusive
d) Rational and logical

159. What did it mean in 16th century England if a black cat appeared on a ship?
a) The ship would have a safe journey
b) Pirates were nearby
c) The ship would sink
d) It would rain the next day

160. In Scotland, seeing a black cat on your doorstep is believed to bring what?
a) A new family member
b) Wealth and prosperity
c) An argument
d) A bad omen

161. In which culture were cats believed to have the ability to guard the afterlife, serving as guides for souls?
a) Greek
b) Roman
c) Egyptian
d) Norse

162. In Buddhism, what is the cat often considered a symbol of?

a) Greed
b) Wisdom
c) Enlightenment
d) Laziness

163. In France, what is it said to mean if a cat sneezes on your wedding day?
a) The marriage will be prosperous
b) You will have bad luck
c) A storm is coming
d) Your marriage will end soon

164. Which ancient culture linked cats with the moon and its cycles, often viewing them as lunar creatures?

a) Greek
b) Celtic
c) Egyptian
d) Norse

165. In astrology, which planet is most closely associated with cats due to their mystery and independence?
a) Mercury
b) Venus
c) Uranus
d) Saturn

166. In which country is it considered you're going to come down with a cold if a cat sneezes three times?
a) France
b) Italy
c) China
d) Australia

167. According to Russian folklore, what is the significance of letting a cat enter a new home before the owners?
a) The cat blesses the house with prosperity
b) The cat removes bad energy
c) The cat decides if the house is haunted
d) The cat ensures fertility

168. In which culture is it believed that a cat sleeping on a sick person's bed can predict their death?
a) Norwegian
b) Chinese
c) Jewish
d) Irish

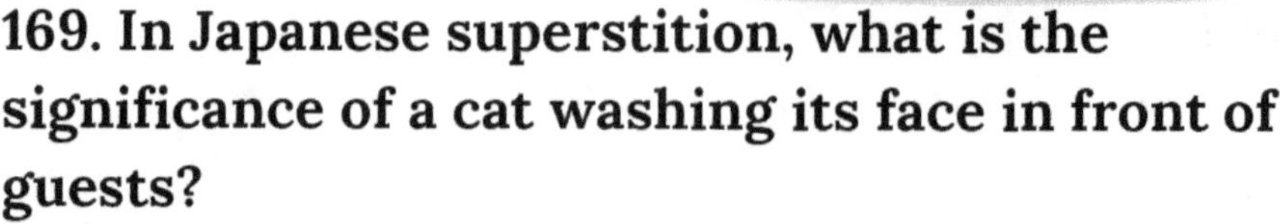

169. In Japanese superstition, what is the significance of a cat washing its face in front of guests?
a) It foretells rain

b) It means good luck is on the way
c) It signals a financial loss
d) It indicates the guests will leave soon

170. In ancient Egypt, what was believed to happen if a cat walked through a house during a funeral procession?
a) The soul of the deceased would find peace
b) The deceased would be reincarnated as a cat
c) The deceased would be cursed
d) The spirit of the deceased would linger

171. In which country is it believed that feeding a cat first during dinner can bring financial success?
a) Mexico
b) Greece
c) Thailand
d) Brazil

172. In Latvian folklore, what does it mean when a cat jumps on the cradle of a newborn?
a) The child will be wealthy
b) The child will be cursed
c) The child will grow up to be a musician
d) The child will marry young

173. In Finnish superstition, what was it believed

that cats could do to babies if left alone with them?
a) Take their breath away
b) Steal their souls
c) Protect them from evil spirits
d) Bring them good dreams

174. In Polish culture, what does a cat rubbing against someone's leg indicate?
a) You will soon receive money
b) You are being protected from a curse
c) Bad weather is coming
d) Someone is gossiping about you

175. In medieval European superstition, what was a common belief about cats and pregnant women?
a) Cats could steal the baby's soul
b) Cats were protectors of pregnant women
c) Cats caused infertility
d) Cats could predict the baby's gender

Chapter 7: The Language of Cats

176. What type of vocalization do cats commonly use to communicate with each other during mating season?

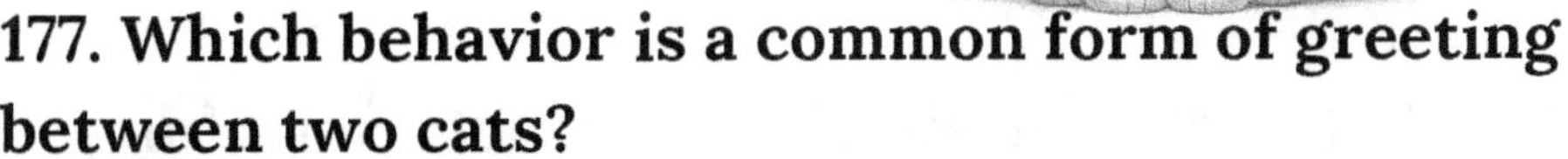

a) Purring
b) Meowing
c) Yowling
d) Chirping

177. Which behavior is a common form of greeting between two cats?

a) Hissing
b) Head bumping
c) Staring
d) Hiding

178. What does it mean when one cat grooms another?

a) They are marking territory
b) They are showing dominance
c) They are establishing social bonds
d) They are preparing to mate

179. When two cats engage in "slow blinking" toward each other, what is this generally interpreted as?

a) Aggression
b) A sign of trust
c) A challenge
d) Curiosity

180. What does a cat's short, high-pitched meow usually signify?

a) Hunger
b) Pain
c) Fear
d) A greeting

181. What does it mean when a cat lets out a long, drawn-out meow?

a) They are sick
b) They are asking for attention or food
c) They are angry
d) They are warning of danger

182. What might a loud, continuous purr indicate when a cat is near a human?

a) The cat is ready to play
b) The cat is anxious
c) The cat is seeking comfort or reassurance

d) The cat is in pain

183. How can you distinguish a "happy" purr from a "distress" purr?
a) By the speed of the purring
b) By the pitch of the purring
c) By the duration of the purring
d) By the volume of the purring

184. When a cat's tail is slowly moving back and forth, what does this generally indicate?
a) Playfulness
b) Aggression
c) Fear
d) Relaxation

185. If a cat's tail is low and twitching at the tip, what might this indicate?
a) Playfulness
b) Annoyance or irritation
c) Confidence
d) Fear

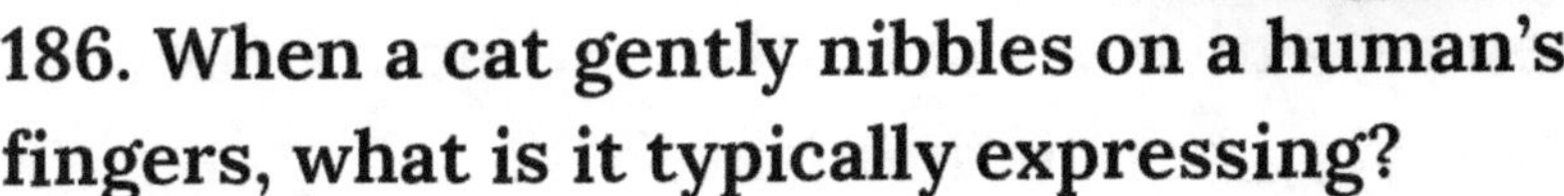

186. When a cat gently nibbles on a human's fingers, what is it typically expressing?
a) Affection
b) Fear

c) Hunger
d) Anger

187. What might a cat be communicating by following its human around the house?
a) Curiosity
b) Loneliness or a desire for attention
c) Hunger
d) A territorial warning

188. When a cat "head bunts" or presses its head against a person, what is it doing?
a) Marking its territory with scent
b) Showing anger
c) Asking to be fed
d) Displaying dominance

189. What does it mean when two cats touch noses?
a) They are challenging each other
b) They are greeting one another
c) They are afraid of each other
d) They are trying to avoid conflict

190. When cats hiss at each other, what are they generally trying to communicate?
a) Aggression and fear
b) Playfulness

c) Hunger
d) Curiosity

191. What is the typical reason for cats to arch their backs when meeting another cat?
a) They are ready to play
b) They are attempting to look bigger to scare the other cat
c) They are stretching
d) They are marking territory

192. When a cat rolls over and exposes its belly to another cat, what does it signify?
a) Submission
b) Aggression
c) Playfulness
d) Trust

193. Which type of vocalization might a cat make when excited or curious, particularly when watching birds or insects?
a) Trilling
b) Yowling
c) Chattering
d) Growling

194. Cats will often emit a soft, short "mew" sound

when they are feeling:
a) Threatened
b) Playful
c) Annoyed
d) Afraid

195. What does a rapid, high-pitched "trill" typically indicate when a cat communicates with humans?
a) The cat is trying to scold you
b) The cat is hungry
c) The cat is excited or happy
d) The cat is ready to fight

Chapter 8: Cats and Their Relationships with Other Animals

196. What is one of the main reasons why cats and dogs may not get along?
a) Different diets
b) Different body language
c) Different sleeping habits
d) Different grooming routines

197. In what type of household environment are cats and dogs more likely to form friendships?
a) When they are raised together from a young age
b) When they are of the same gender
c) When they have the same fur color
d) When they have the same sleeping patterns

198. How do cats often show dominance over dogs in a shared home?
a) By eating the dog's food
b) By lying in higher places
c) By barking loudly
d) By sleeping more often

199. What kind of play behavior is common between cats and dogs that indicates a friendly relationship?
a) Chasing and pouncing
b) Sleeping in separate rooms
c) Ignoring each other completely
d) Scratching furniture together

200. What does it mean when a cat hisses at a dog?
a) The cat is inviting the dog to play
b) The cat is warning the dog to stay away
c) The cat is hungry
d) The cat is protecting its territory

201. Why might a cat swat at a dog without using its claws?
a) As a form of friendly play
b) As a sign of affection
c) To show irritation without causing harm
d) To initiate a fight

202. What breed of dog is known for being particularly good at getting along with cats?
a) Chihuahua
b) Golden Retriever
c) Bulldog
d) German Shepherd

203. Which behavior indicates that a cat feels comfortable around a dog?
a) Lying down and exposing its belly
b) Keeping its tail low and tucked
c) Avoiding eye contact
d) Running away when the dog approaches

204. What is one way to help a cat and dog form a friendship in a multi-pet household?
a) Feed them together from the same bowl
b) Provide separate spaces for each animal
c) Force them to share the same bed
d) Ignore their interactions

205. What percentage of a domestic cat's diet is made up of small animals like birds, in the wild?
a) 30%
b) 50%
c) 70%
d) 90%

206. What behavior might a cat exhibit when watching birds through a window?
a) Yawning
b) Tail flicking and chattering
c) Sleeping
d) Purring

207. In which region have domestic cats contributed to the extinction of many bird species?
a) Australia
b) Europe
c) South America
d) Antarctica

208. What is one of the best ways to prevent a domestic cat from hunting birds?
a) Feed the cat more frequently
b) Keep the cat indoors
c) Yell at the cat when it catches birds
d) Play loud music outside

209. What type of collar can be used to warn birds of a cat's presence?
a) A bell collar
b) A leather collar
c) A reflective collar
d) A collar with feathers

210. What does it mean when a cat "chirps" while looking at a bird?
a) It is frustrated it can't reach the bird
b) It is calling to the bird
c) It is confused
d) It is scared

211. What instinctual behavior drives a cat to hunt birds?
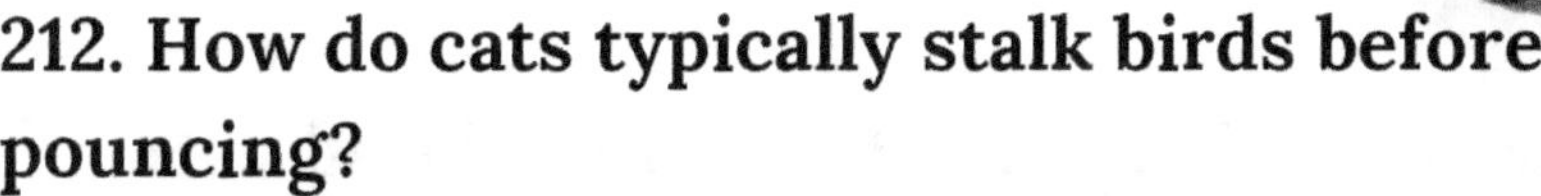
a) Its sense of adventure
b) Its need for exercise
c) Its natural predatory instinct
d) Its boredom

212. How do cats typically stalk birds before pouncing?
a) By walking in circles around them
b) By lying low to the ground and moving slowly
c) By running quickly toward them
d) By meowing loudly to distract them

213. What time of day are cats most likely to hunt birds?
a) Morning and evening (dawn and dusk)
b) Midday
c) Late at night
d) Early afternoon

214. What behavior might a cat show when it forms a bond with an animal of a different species?
a) Grooming the other animal
b) Hiding from the other animal
c) Hissing at the other animal
d) Ignoring the other animal

215. Which big cat species has been observed forming bonds with humans or animals of different species in captivity?
a) Lion
b) Tiger
c) Cheetah
d) Leopard

216. How do motherless kittens often bond with animals of other species?
a) By mimicking their behaviors
b) By grooming them
c) By sleeping next to them
d) By following them everywhere

217. What is a common reason why cats develop friendly relationships with animals from different species?
a) The animals have shared experiences
b) The cat is lonely
c) The cat is protecting its territory
d) The cat has been trained to do so

Chapter 9: Cats in Art, Fashion, and Design

218. Which famous Spanish artist often featured cats in his surrealist paintings, including his 1939 piece "The Enigma of Hitler"?
a) Pablo Picasso
b) Salvador Dalí
c) Joan Miró
d) Diego Rivera

219. What French painter is known for his iconic posters of cats, including the famous "Le Chat Noir" cabaret advertisement?
a) Henri de Toulouse-Lautrec
b) Théophile Steinlen
c) Edgar Degas
d) Claude Monet

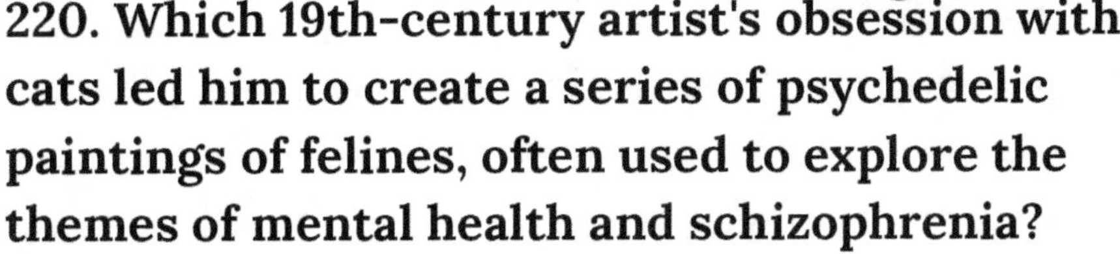

220. Which 19th-century artist's obsession with cats led him to create a series of psychedelic paintings of felines, often used to explore the themes of mental health and schizophrenia?
a) Louis Wain

b) Gustave Courbet
c) Edouard Manet
d) Vincent van Gogh

221. Which illustrator, known for The Church Mice series, created a world where mice and a friendly cat named Sam go on adventures together?
a) Garth Williams
b) Graham Oakley
c) Edward Ardizzone
d) Maurice Sendak

222. In Ghirlandaio's The Last Supper, what does the cat sitting at Judas's feet symbolize within the context of the painting?
a) Innocence
b) Betrayal
c) Protection
d) Wealth

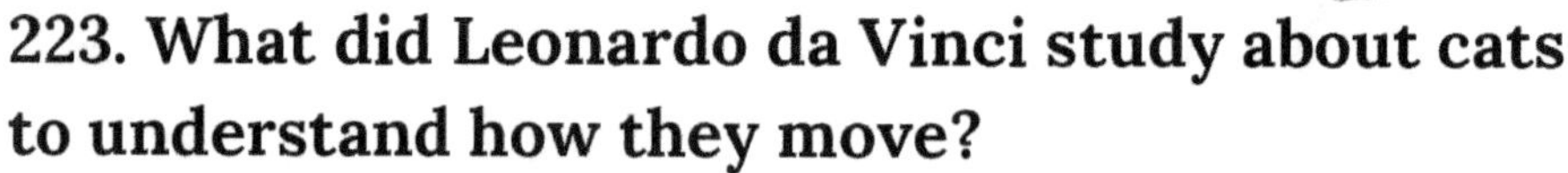

223. What did Leonardo da Vinci study about cats to understand how they move?
a) Their sleeping habits
b) Their anatomy and muscle movements
c) Their diet
d) Their social behavior

224. Which French Impressionist artist painted "Julie Manet with Cat," a tender portrait of a young girl holding her pet cat?
a) Pierre-Auguste Renoir
b) Edgar Degas
c) Édouard Manet
d) Camille Pissarro

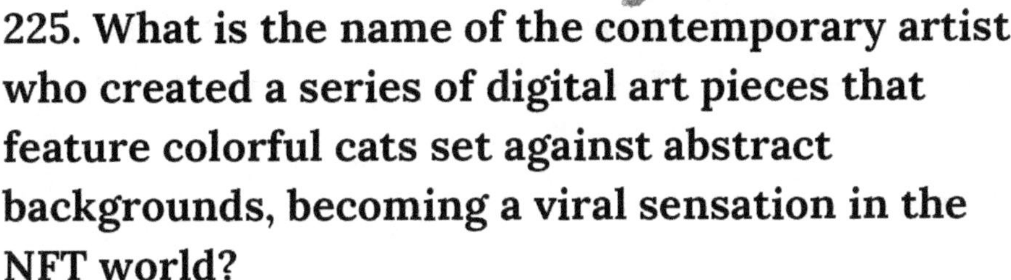

225. What is the name of the contemporary artist who created a series of digital art pieces that feature colorful cats set against abstract backgrounds, becoming a viral sensation in the NFT world?
a) Beeple
b) XCOPY
c) Takashi Murakami
d) Banksy

226. Which luxury fashion brand frequently incorporates cat motifs into its designs, including cat-shaped handbags and feline-inspired prints?
a) Chanel
b) Gucci
c) Versace
d) Prada

227. What famous fashion designer, known for his

love of cats, often featured his white Birman cat, Choupette, as a muse for his work?
a) Giorgio Armani
b) Karl Lagerfeld
c) Ralph Lauren
d) Marc Jacobs

228. Which high-fashion item, inspired by the flexible and sleek movements of cats, was first popularized in the 1960s by designer Yves Saint Laurent?
a) Jumpsuit
b) Catsuit
c) Mini skirt
d) Peacoat

229. In which decade did leopard print, a pattern often associated with the grace and power of wild cats, become a staple in women's fashion?
a) 1940s
b) 1960s
c) 1980s
d) 2000s

230. Which pop star famously performed wearing a rhinestone-studded catsuit during her "Dangerously in Love" tour in 2003?

a) Britney Spears
b) Beyoncé
c) Christina Aguilera
d) Lady Gaga

231. What animal-inspired makeup trend, involving a dramatic winged eyeliner, became synonymous with feline elegance and has remained popular since the 1950s?
a) Smoky eye
b) Cat-eye makeup
c) Bold lipstick
d) Natural look

232. Which Italian designer brand played on the term catwalk, using cat-faced avatar models to showcase their collection at the Metaverse Fashion Week?
a) Dolce & Gabbana
b) Versace
c) Fendi
d) Moschino

233. Where and when was the world's first cat café established?
a) Tokyo, 2000
b) Taipei, 1998

c) Seoul, 2005
d) Vienna, 2012

234. Which city is home to the oldest cat café in Europe, opening its doors in 2012?
a) Paris
b) Vienna
c) Berlin
d) London

235. What term describes the act of paying for time to interact with cats in a relaxed café setting, a trend that has grown popular globally?
a) Cat therapy
b) Cat yoga
c) Feline experience
d) Purr therapy

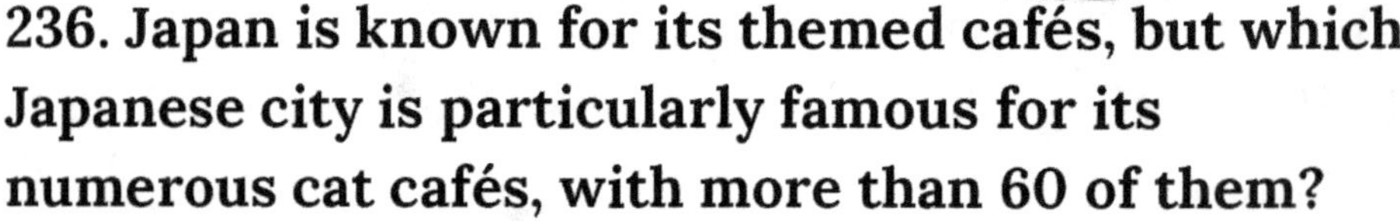

236. Japan is known for its themed cafés, but which Japanese city is particularly famous for its numerous cat cafés, with more than 60 of them?
a) Kyoto
b) Osaka
c) Yokohama
d) Tokyo

237. In which North American city did the first

official cat café, "Cat Town Café," open in 2014?
a) Seattle
b) San Francisco
c) Oakland
d) New York

238. What is the name of the first cat café to open in New York City, established in 2014 as a pop-up before becoming permanent?
a) Cat Café NYC
b) Meow Parlour
c) Purr Café
d) Cat Lounge

239. What primary benefit do cat cafés promote, aside from coffee and snacks, that encourages frequent visits from cat lovers?
a) Networking opportunities
b) Stress relief
c) Cat grooming services
d) Yoga classes

240. In South Korea, what is the local term for cat cafés, where cats freely roam and interact with visitors?
a) Goyangi café
b) Cat lounge

c) Neko café
d) Meow café

241. Which popular home décor item features cats and has become a favorite among cat lovers, often found on beds, couches and armchairs?
a) Cat figurines
b) Cat wall art
c) Cat-themed throw pillows
d) Cat rugs

242. What is the name of the trend where cat owners design their homes to include cat-friendly furniture, such as cat trees and shelves?
a) Feline-friendly design
b) Cat chic
c) Catification
d) Meow décor

243. Which type of home accessory, often featuring cat faces or silhouettes, became popular in the 2010s as a whimsical addition to kitchens?
a) Cat mugs
b) Cat oven mitts
c) Cat coasters
d) Cat aprons

244. Which home décor brand, known for its playful cat-themed items, offers everything from furniture to kitchenware for cat lovers?
a) Zazzle
b) Cat studio
c) Urban Outfitters
d) Anthropologie

Chapter 10: Fun Facts You Probably Didn't Know

245. What is the traditional Japanese cat figurine known as that is believed to bring good luck?
a) Kawaii
b) Maneki-Neko
c) Neko-Chan
d) Inu-Tama

246. In Japanese culture, what does the left paw raised in a Maneki-Neko figurine represent?
a) Attracting customers
b) Good fortune
c) Protection
d) Love

247. In which Japanese city can you find the famous "Cat Temple" known as Gotokuji, which features hundreds of Maneki-Neko?
a) Kyoto
b) Osaka
c) Tokyo
d) Hiroshima

248. What unique cat-themed festival takes place annually in Japan, celebrating the bond between cats and their owners?
a) Cat Day
b) Cats and Owners
c) Neko Matsuri
d) Cat Lovers' Day

249. Which Japanese island is known for its large population of cats, outnumbering humans by more than six to one?
a) Tashirojima
b) Aoshima
c) Okishima
d) Nekojima

250. In which country did the government introduce a law in June 2024 that makes it mandatory to microchip cats?
a) France
b) Germany
c) United Kingdom
d) Canada

251. Which U.S. state was the first to pass a law requiring pet shops to only sell cats and dogs from shelters?

a) California
b) New york
c) Florida
d) Texas

252. Which European country has laws in place that allow residents to sue their neighbors if their cats cause damage to their property?
a) Norway
b) Sweden
c) Denmark
d) Netherlands

253. Which city is known for its large population of stray cats and the famous Cat Island located nearby?
a) Rome
b) Istanbul
c) Athens
d) New York

254. Which U.S. city has a cat rescue organization called "The Cat House on the Kings" that is one of the largest no-cage cat sanctuaries in the country?
a) San Francisco
b) Los Angeles
c) Fresno
d) Seattle

255. In which city can you find the famous Cat Museum, dedicated to the love and history of cats, located in the heart of the city?
a) Bucharest
b) Lisbon
c) Kuala Lumpur
d) Sydney

256. What city in the United States hosted the 2024 "CatCon" event, celebrating all things cat-related with vendors, art, and rescue organizations?
a) Austin
b) Los Angeles
c) New York
d) Chicago

257. What percentage of a cat's brain is dedicated to memory?
a) 25%
b) 50%
c) 70%
d) 90%

258. What unique ability do cats possess that allows them to always land on their feet?
a) Flexible spine
b) Quick reflexes

c) Righting reflex
d) Strong legs

259. What is the term for a group of cats?
a) A clowder
b) A gaggle
c) A pack
d) A colony

260. How many vocal sounds can a cat make, allowing them to communicate with humans and other cats?
a) 10
b) 30
c) 100
d) 50

261. Which part of a cat's body contains a high concentration of scent glands?
a) Ears
b) Paws
c) Whiskers
d) Face

262. What percentage of a cat's DNA is shared with humans?
a) 25%

b) 50%
c) 60%
d) 90%

263. What is the average lifespan of an indoor cat?

a) 5-10 years
b) 10-15 years
c) 15-20 years
d) 20-25 years

264. What special ability do cats have that allows them to detect changes in the environment, such as earthquakes?

a) Acute hearing
b) Strong intuition
c) Enhanced smell
d) Vibration sensitivity

265. How many toes do most cats have on their front paws?

a) 4
b) 5
c) 6
d) 7

266. What is the scientific name for the domestic cat?

a) Felis catus
b) Felis domestica
c) Felis silvestris
d) Felis leo

267. Why do cats often knock things off tables for no apparent reason?

a) They're testing gravity
b) They enjoy watching things fall
c) They're practicing their hunting skills
d) They want your attention

268. Why do cats love to squeeze into small boxes or containers?

a) They're secretly practicing for magic shows
b) They feel safe and cozy in tight spaces
c) They want to be as small as possible
d) They're defying the laws of physics

269. What's the main reason cats love to perch on high places?

a) They like to pretend they're royalty
b) They're surveying their kingdom
c) They're judging your interior design choices
d) They enjoy feeling superior

270. What is the real reason cats love to "help"

when you're trying to wrap gifts?
a) They're practicing their gift-wrapping skills
b) They love the sound of crinkling paper
c) They think you need extra paws to do the job right
d) They're secretly trying to steal the ribbon

Chapter 11: Caring for Your Cat

271. What is the best type of food to provide a well-balanced diet for your cat?
a) Dry food only
b) Wet food only
c) A mix of wet and dry food
d) Homemade meals

272. Which nutrient is essential for cats but not for dogs?
a) Taurine
b) Vitamin C
c) Carbohydrates
d) Iron

273. How often should adult cats typically be fed?
a) Once a day
b) Twice a day
c) Three times a day
d) Free feeding all day

274. What type of food should be avoided in a cat's

diet due to the risk of toxicity?

a) Tuna
b) Milk
c) Chocolate
d) Carrots

275. What is a key sign that your cat may be overeating?

a) Constant meowing
b) Visible weight gain
c) Sleeping more
d) Drinking more water

276. How often should short-haired cats typically be brushed?

a) Once a month
b) Once a week
c) Every day
d) Every two weeks

277. What is the best way to prevent hairballs in cats?

a) Bathing them regularly
b) Brushing them often
c) Feeding them dry food
d) Limiting their grooming habits

278. Why is it important to regularly trim your cat's nails?
a) To prevent scratching furniture
b) To reduce the risk of infection
c) To keep their claws sharp
d) To help them climb better

279. What kind of brush is most recommended for long-haired cats?
a) Slicker brush
b) Rubber brush
c) Bristle brush
d) Comb

280. How often should you bathe your cat?
a) Every week
b) Every month
c) Only when necessary
d) Every three months

281. What is the most important feature to include in a cat-friendly home?
a) A scratching post
b) Lots of plants
c) A large bed
d) Bright lights

282. Why should you provide vertical spaces like shelves or cat trees for your cat?

a) To encourage climbing
b) To make the home look stylish
c) To help them relax
d) To improve their sense of balance

283. What type of litter box is best for multi-cat households?

a) One large litter box
b) Multiple litter boxes in different areas
c) Self-cleaning litter box
d) Covered litter box

284. How often should you clean your cat's litter box?

a) Once a day
b) Twice a week
c) Every other day
d) Once a week

285. What is a good way to keep indoor cats stimulated?

a) Allowing them to watch birds from the window
b) Giving them plenty of naps
c) Letting them roam outside alone
d) Playing soothing music

286. Why should you avoid using harsh chemicals in your home around cats?
a) Cats dislike strong smells
b) It can damage their fur
c) Cats are sensitive to toxins
d) It affects their appetite

287. How often should a healthy adult cat visit the veterinarian for a check-up?
a) Once a year
b) Twice a year
c) Every two years
d) Only when they're sick

288. What is the primary benefit of spaying or neutering your cat?
a) It makes them more affectionate
b) It prevents unwanted behaviors
c) It extends their lifespan
d) It prevents overpopulation

289. How can you tell if your cat is feeling stressed?
a) They start purring more
b) They hide or avoid interaction
c) They sleep less
d) They become extra playful

290. What is the most common cause of obesity in cats?

a) Overfeeding
b) Not enough water
c) Too much exercise
d) Feeding them at night

291. Why is regular dental care important for cats?
a) To improve their breath
b) To prevent tooth decay and gum disease
c) To help them eat more food
d) To reduce fur shedding

292. What is the average heart rate for a healthy cat?
a) 60-90 beats per minute
b) 120-160 beats per minute
c) 140-220 beats per minute
d) 100-120 beats per minute

293. How do cats typically react when their human is feeling stressed or anxious?
a) They run and hide
b) They become more affectionate
c) They ignore them
d) They start meowing loudly

294. Why do some cats choose to sit on people who dislike cats?
a) They sense their fear
b) They want to challenge them
c) Cats like to prove a point
d) They're drawn to non-threatening behavior

295. How do cats respond when their human is sad or crying?
a) They purr loudly
b) They avoid them
c) They may cuddle or stay close
d) They become hyperactive

296. What sense helps cats recognize their human's mood most accurately?
a) Sight
b) Smell
c) Hearing
d) Touch

297. What is one way cats demonstrate problem-solving abilities?
a) Learning to open doors
b) Sleeping in new spots
c) Following commands
d) Ignoring their owners

298. How long can a cat's memory last for certain events or actions?
a) A few minutes
b) Up to 16 hours
c) A few days
d) Several months

299. What is one sign of high intelligence in cats?
a) Staring at a wall for hours
b) Learning to use the toilet
c) Ignoring toys
d) Scratching furniture

300. How do cats often learn behaviors like opening cabinets or turning on faucets?
a) Through observing humans
b) Through trial and error
c) By instinct
d) By imitating other animals

Answers

1. b) Fertile Crescent
2. a) African wildcat (Felis lybica)
3. d) They were drawn to rodents attracted by stored grain
4. c) 9,000 years ago
5. c) The Egyptians
6. a) Bastet
7. b) Cats migrated on their own, traveling across land bridges
8. c) They were primarily hunters of rodents
9. b) Cat burials near human settlements
10. a) A change in brain development genes
11. b) A cat buried alongside a human
12. b) Goddess of protection, fertility, and home
13. c) They protected homes from pests and represented the goddess Bastet
14. c) They could face the death penalty
15. b) By mummifying cats and offering them to the gods
16. c) Bubastis
17. a) Offering food to stray cats
18. c) The Persians used cats on their shields, knowing Egyptians wouldn't harm them

19. a) Linen
20. b) A woman with the head of a cat
21. a) Freyja
22. b) It is considered a witch's familiar and a bad omen
23. c) Maneki-neko
24. c) They are often depicted as shape-shifters
25. c) A legendary cat believed to have magical powers
26. b) A warning of impending danger
27. b) The Phoenicians
28. a) Felicette
29. b) You will soon have a visitor
30. b) It transforms into a powerful spirit known as a bakeneko
31. a) Socks
32. a) Pablo Picasso
33. c) Polydactyl
34. b) Jock
35. c) Mikhail Bulgakov
36. a) 15 minutes
37. c) T.S. Eliot
38. c) Angora
39. c) Charles Dickens
40. c) Colombian ocelot
41. b) Isaac Newton
42. d) Music and cats

43. b) Cubism
44. b) Chippy
45. b) The Cat in the Hat
46. a) Long, flowing coat
47. b) Sphynx
48. c) Long, bushy tail and large size
49. a) Blue eyes and vocal nature
50. a) Scottish Fold
51. b) Calm and floppy nature when picked up
52. a) Maine Coon
53. a) Speckled or marbled coat resembling wild cats
54. a) Ticked coat (agouti)
55. a) Munchkin
56. b) Serval
57. a) It has a wolf-like appearance due to partial hair loss
58. d) Selkirk Rex
59. a) Swimming
60. a) Naturally short "pom-pom" tail
61. c) African Serval
62. a) Thailand
63. a) It has no outer coat, just soft, wavy undercoat
64. c) Chausie
65. a) Scandinavia
66. a) Thailand (formerly Siam)
67. a) Turkey
68. c) Birman
69. a) France

70. a) Chartreux

71. a) Russia

72. a) England

73. a) Large, round cheeks

74. a) It has a curly, springy texture

75. a) Black panther

76. a) 200 degrees

77. d) A reflective layer behind their retina called the tapetum lucidum

78. c) Blue and gray

79. b) To control the amount of light entering their eyes

80. b) Cats have excellent depth perception due to their forward-facing eyes

81. b) 25-150 Hz

82. d) All of the above

83. b) False

84. b) Purring helps in healing bones and tissues

85. c) To bond with their mother while nursing

86. a) Vibrissae

87. b) Detecting nearby objects and movements

88. b) 12

89. d) On their forelegs

90. a) True

91. b) Confidence and friendliness

92. a) It's a way of marking territory

93. c) The cat is frightened or angry
94. b) As a gift or offering
95. c) The cat is showing trust and affection
96. b) 12-16 hours
97. a) To conserve energy for hunting
98. d) Cat nap
99. a) Twitch their paws and whiskers
100. b) They sleep more as they get older
101. c) Dr. Seuss
102. b) A trickster who helps his master rise to wealth and power
103. a) Cheshire Cat
104. a) Edgar Allan Poe
105. a) Cats
106. b) The Cat (it is unnamed)
107. a) Cats that form clans
108. a) Crookshanks
109. c) Pink and purple stripes
110. b) He ruins his clothes and gets scolded
111. c) Garfield
112. c) A mouse named Jerry
113. c) Sylvester
114. b) Black and white
115. c) The Itchy & Scratchy Show
116. a) Stray alley cat
117. a) Duchess
118. a) Tardar Sauce
119. b) Nyan Cat

120. d) Lil BUB
121. a) Japan
122. c) Grumpy Cat
123. b) Maru
124. b) Tabby
125. a) Creme Puff
126. b) Savannah
127. b) 21.3 kg (46.8 lbs)
128. a) Singapura
129. c) 123 cm (48.5 in)
130. c) Ashera
131. c) 420
132. b) 19 kittens
133. b) Siamese
134. a) 16 years old
135. a) Colonel Meow
136. b) 26 tricks
137. a) Smokey
138. b) 67.8 dB
139. a) Waffle
140. b) Nala
141. c) Japan
142. a) Irish
143. a) Sacred and protective
144. a) Good fortune is on its way
145. a) Sailors
146. b) Witches in disguise

147. c) Witches' Sabbaths
148. b) Cats
149. a) Cat Sidhe
150. c) Ghosts
151. a) Japanese
152. d) Latvia
153. a) Prophet Muhammad
154. a) Rabbit
155. a) Leo
156. b) Sekhmet
157. a) Water
158. b) Bold and confident
159. a) The ship would have a safe journey
160. b) Wealth and prosperity
161. c) Egyptian
162. b) Wisdom
163. a) The marriage will be prosperous1
164. b) Celtic
165. d) Saturn
166. b) Italy
167. b) The cat removes bad energy
168. d) Irish
169. a) It foretells rain
170. d) The spirit of the deceased would linger
171. a) Mexico
172. c) The child will grow up to be a musician
173. a) Take their breath away
174. d) Someone is gossiping about you

175. a) Cats could steal the baby's soul
176. c) Yowling
177. b) Head bumping
178. c) They are establishing social bonds
179. b) A sign of trust
180. d) A greeting
181. b) They are asking for attention or food
182. c) The cat is seeking comfort or reassurance
183. b) By the pitch of the purring
184. a) Playfulness
185. b) Annoyance or irritation
186. a) Affection
187. b) Loneliness or a desire for attention
188. a) Marking its territory with scent
189. b) They are greeting one another
190. a) Aggression and fear
191. b) They are attempting to look bigger to scare
the other cat
192. d) Trust
193. c) Chattering
194. b) Playful
195. c) The cat is excited or happy
196. b) Different body language
197. a) When they are raised together from a young
age
198. b) By lying in higher places
199. a) Chasing and pouncing

200. b) The cat is warning the dog to stay away
201. c) To show irritation without causing harm
202. b) Golden Retriever
203. a) Lying down and exposing its belly
204. b) Provide separate spaces for each animal
205. d) 90%
206. b) Tail flicking and chattering
207. a) Australia
208. b) Keep the cat indoors
209. a) A bell collar
210. a) It is frustrated it can't reach the bird
211. c) Its natural predatory instinct
212. b) By lying low to the ground and moving slowly
213. a) Morning and evening (dawn and dusk)
214. a) Grooming the other animal
215. c) Cheetah
216. c) By sleeping next to them
217. b) The cat is lonely
218. b) Salvador Dalí
219. b) Théophile Steinlen
220. a) Louis Wain
221. b) Graham Oakley
222. b) Betrayal
223. b) Their anatomy and muscle movement
224. a) Pierre-Auguste Renoir
225. b) XCOPY
226. b) Gucci
227. b) Karl Lagerfeld

228. b) Catsuit
229. b) 1960s
230. b) Beyoncé
231. b) Cat-eye makeup
232. a) Dolce & Gabbana
233. b) Taipei, 1998
234. b) Vienna
235. a) Cat therapy
236. d) Tokyo
237. c) Oakland
238. b) Meow Parlour
239. b) Stress relief
240. a) Goyangi café
241. c) Cat-themed throw pillows
242. c) Catification
243. b) Cat oven mitts
244. b) Cat studio
245. b) Maneki-Neko
246. a) Attracting customers
247. c) Tokyo
248. c) Neko Matsuri
249. b) Aoshima
250. c) United Kingdom
251. a) California
252. d) Netherlands
253. b) Istanbul
254. c) Fresno

255. c) Kuala Lumpur
256. b) Los Angeles
257. c) 70%
258. c) Righting reflex
259. a) A clowder
260. c) 100
261. d) Face
262. d) 90%
263. c) 15-20 years
264. d) Vibration sensitivity
265. b) 5
266. a) Felis catus
267. d) They want your attention
268. b) They feel safe and cozy in tight spaces
269. b) They're surveying their kingdom
270. b) They love the sound of crinkling paper
271. c) A mix of wet and dry food
272. a) Taurine
273. b) Twice a day
274. c) Chocolate
275. b) Visible weight gain
276. b) Once a week
277. b) Brushing them often
278. a) To prevent scratching furniture
279. a) Slicker brush
280. c) Only when necessary
281. a) A scratching post
282. a) To encourage climbing

283. b) Multiple litter boxes in different areas
284. a) Once a day
285. a) Allowing them to watch birds from the window
286. c) Cats are sensitive to toxins
287. a) Once a year
288. d) It prevents overpopulation
289. b) They hide or avoid interaction
290. a) Overfeeding
291. b) To prevent tooth decay and gum disease
292. c) 140-220 beats per minute
293. b) They become more affectionate
294. d) They're drawn to non-threatening behavior
295. c) They may cuddle or stay close
296. c) Hearing
297. a) Learning to open doors
298. b) Up to 16 hours
299. b) Learning to use the toilet
300. a) Through observing humans

THE END

Cats have captivated human hearts for thousands of years, weaving themselves into our lives, cultures, and homes with an unspoken grace and charm. The bond between cats and humans is truly special. Whether curled up on our laps, chasing imaginary prey, or quietly observing life from a windowsill, cats bring a sense of companionship unique to their nature. Unlike many pets, cats don't demand constant attention, but their presence is always felt—offering comfort and joy in subtle ways.

This trivia book is a tribute to the remarkable relationship between cats and their human companions. From their mysterious behaviors to their cultural significance, cats prove time and again that they are more than just pets—they are family. Whether you're a lifelong cat lover or new to the world of felines, may this book inspire you to cherish the quirks, love, and joy cats bring to our lives.

After all, the world is a better place with a cat by your side.